# Storm Chasers

# Storm Chasers

**Trudi Strain Trueit**

**Franklin Watts**
A Division of Scholastic Inc.
New York • Toronto • London • Auckland • Sydney
Mexico City • New Delhi • Hong Kong
Danbury, Connecticut

*For my grandfather, Elmus Strain, who always has a thrilling twister tale.*
*And for everyone else who wishes they did.*

**Note to readers:** Definitions for words in **bold** can be found in the Glossary at the back of this book.

Photographs ©: Charles Edwards/Cloud 9 Tours: 34; Corbis-Bettmann: 47 (Reuters NewMedia Inc.), 2; National Geographic Image Collection: 40 (Paul Chesley), 33, 48 (Chris Johns); Photo Researchers, NY: cover, 20, 21, 23, 35 (Howard B. Bluestein), 38 (NASA/Goddard/SPL); Photri: 5 left, 43; Silver Image/James Kamp: 8, 45; Stone/Alan R. Moller: 6, 18; Tom Bean: 10, 19; Tom Pantages/NOAA: 22; Unicorn Stock Photos/Jean Higgins: 12; Weatherstock Inc./Warren Faidley: 5 right, 13, 15, 16, 27 bottom, 27 top, 28, 30, 31, 36, 41, 26 (NOAA).

**Library of Congress Cataloging-in-Publication Data**

Trueit, Trudi Strain.
    Storm chasers / Trudi Strain Trueit.
       p.      cm. — (Watts Library)
    Includes bibliographical references and index.
    ISBN 0-531-11971-8 (lib. bdg.)     0-531-16219-2 (pbk.)
    1. Severe storms—Juvenile literature. [1. Tornadoes. 2. Hurricanes.] I. Title. II. Series.
QC944.2 .T78 2001
551.55'3—dc21
2001017572

# Contents

*Tornadoes arrive suddenly and reduce everything in their path to splinters. This twister ravaged a town in Texas in 1995.*

# Storm Struck

**Tornadoes** are some of Earth's most unpredictable and least understood storms. In a matter of minutes, a twister can touch down to toss cars in the air and shred buildings, then vanish as quickly as it appeared. It can roar through a neighborhood, ripping apart homes on one side of the street while leaving those on the other side completely untouched.

Tornadoes fascinate us even as they frighten us. Since 1939, audiences have been spellbound by the mighty whirlwind that swallowed Dorothy in *The Wizard of Oz*. The 1996 movie *Twister* sparked interest not only in tornadoes, but also in the people who dare to venture near them. Every year, thousands of tourists flock to Wakita, Oklahoma, to tour the *Twister* Museum and movie location. Others plan their summer vacations around storm-chasing adventure tours scattered throughout **Tornado Alley** in the Central Plains.

The growing interest in tornadoes has also brought some danger. Some people who watch storm chasing on television or in the movies decide to try it themselves. Many of these amateur chasers, however, have not studied **meteorology**, the science of weather. They have not learned safety measures, and as a result, they drive too fast or get too close to storms.

*A meteorologist charts tropical storms at the National Hurricane Center in Florida.*

Some have even been hit by lightning! Amateur chasers put both themselves and others at risk.

When it comes to sheer power and size, no storm on Earth can match a **hurricane**. Born over warm waters, these mighty storms steam toward land with winds topping 150 miles (240 kilometers) per hour, dangerous lightning and thunder, heavy rains, and gigantic waves. Hurricanes have storm chasers of their own. The Hurricane Hunters, members of the U.S. Air Force Reserve's 53rd Weather Reconnaissance Squadron, are charged with flying into the midst of tropical storms to gather information for scientists and forecasters.

In this book, we will peer into some of nature's deadliest creations through the eyes of the trained people who explore them. While you might be curious about severe storms, always remember to leave the chasing to the professionals. Keep your distance, keep safe, and keep reading!

Storm chasers watch as low, dark clouds race across the sky in the muggy air. This is tornado weather.

# Chapter One

# Tailing Tornadoes

It is just after dawn in Norman, Oklahoma, when Greg Stumpf steps outside to read the sky. A low layer of broken gray clouds races northward. On the ground, the air is muggy with barely a breeze. All signs point to a day of wild weather ahead. Greg is a **storm chaser**, and it is time for the hunt.

Greg is a meteorologist, a scientist who studies weather, and he works for the National Severe Storms Laboratory (NSSL). He has tracked tornadoes, also called twisters, for more than fifteen years. For most people, tailing storms is not a full-time job. Many chasers, like Greg, are meteorologists who follow storms in their spare time or chase together as part of a research team. Although storm chasing can be exciting, Greg's main goal is to help people learn more about these raging columns of wind.

It is late May, the height of chase season in Tornado Alley, a region in central North America that sees more tornado activity than anywhere else in the world. Tornado Alley stretches north from Texas to Nebraska, northeast to Ohio, and into Canada. Greg is in the best place at the best time to spot a tornado, but there are no guarantees he will see one today. There never are.

## Storm Strategy

After his quick survey of the early morning sky, Greg logs on to his computer to check weather conditions from the **radiosondes**. A radiosonde, also called a weather balloon, is a package of weather sensors attached to a helium-filled balloon. As the radiosonde rises, it sends information about **humidity** (the amount of moisture in the air), temperature, and winds to meteorologists at the

*A radiosonde, or weather balloon, sends information about humidity, temperature, and wind speed to meteorologists.*

*Supercells, severe thunderstorms that last for an hour or more, can spawn tornadoes.*

National Weather Service (NWS). Eventually, the balloon bursts, and the radiosonde parachutes to the ground.

Today, the radiosondes are showing plenty of **wind shear**. This condition occurs when winds blow from opposing directions at different heights. As it gets the air spinning in a **thunderstorm**, wind shear creates the right conditions for a tornado to form.

Greg also notes that the air above 20,000 feet (6,000 meters) is cold, while temperatures closer to the ground are warm. This is another clue that stormy weather is coming. On the **weather satellite** photograph, Greg spots a **dry line** of thunderclouds about 100 miles (160 km) west of Norman.

### Weather Watchers

During the peak tornado-sighting months of May and June, up to two hundred chasers are on the road each day.

13

**Right Recipe**

Of the 100,000 thunderstorms that strike the United States each year, less than 1 percent—about 1,000—creates a tornado.

This line is where cool, dry air from the west meets warm, moist air coming north from the Gulf of Mexico. The cool air slides underneath the warmer air, which rises upward to create **cumulonimbus clouds**, or thunderheads. The strongest thunderstorms, known as **supercells**, frequently occur along a dry line. Supercells are the most likely storms to give birth to tornadoes.

Greg searches the weather data for a place where the tip of the moisture from the gulf crosses the dry line. He finds this target area about 50 miles (80 km) south of Wichita Falls, Texas. Checking in with the Storm Prediction Center (SPC) in Norman, Greg discovers that the National Weather Service agrees with him. Now it's time to hit the road.

## The Chase

Greg has packed his gear days ahead of time. In his car he carries a camera, camcorder, cellular phone, portable radio, shortwave ham radio (for communicating with other chasers), charged batteries, and a laptop computer for downloading weather data. Chasers can photograph storms digitally and transfer the photos onto the Internet right in the middle of a chase.

Before he heads for the target area, Greg stops to fill his gas tank and pick up a friend. It is much safer to chase in pairs. Bill Martin, also an experienced chaser, reads the map and weather data while Greg drives. Along the way, they listen to conversations on the ham radio between NWS and Skywarn storm

*Storm chasers pack their equipment days ahead of time. Necessities include a cell phone, shortwave radio, camera, and batteries.*

spotters, trained volunteers who call in to report severe weather near their homes. Two hours into the journey, there is no trace of a storm, but the team is not discouraged. Greg knows storm chasing is part science, part skill, and plenty of patience. A little luck helps, too—only about one in nine chases will lead to a tornado sighting.

Downloading new weather information onto the laptop, Greg and Bill discover that their target area has moved south toward Olney, Texas. They must change course. Three miles (5 km) outside of Olney, they spot **towers**, cumulonimbus clouds that signal severe thunderstorms. On the radio, the Storm Prediction Center issues a tornado watch for the area. They are getting closer!

## Tornado or Bust

On a typical day, a storm chaser spends about 8 hours in the car driving 500 miles (800 km). Nearly half the time, the chase ends in a bust, meaning no major storm or tornado was spotted.

## Watch or Warning?

A tornado watch means a tornado is possible, while a tornado warning means a twister has been sighted or picked up on radar.

# Danger Zone

Another 10 miles (16 km) down the road, Greg and Bill "go visual," following the storm by sight. The tops of the clouds are flattening out, becoming **anvil clouds**. Wind shear is pushing the clouds in a counterclockwise direction. A super-cell is developing.

Soon, a long, gray **wall cloud** drops from below the storm. A wall cloud, which ranges from 1 to 4 miles (2 to 6 km) wide, is sometimes seen just before a **funnel cloud** forms. Wall clouds only produce tornadoes less than half the time, but Greg and Bill are hoping now is one of those times.

Experience tells the two chasers that the safest place to set up their camera gear is on a hill about 3 miles (5 km) east of

*Dropping from below the storm, a wall cloud alerts chasers to the possibility of a tornado.*

the storm. Tornadoes usually move southwest to northeast at an average speed of 30 miles (50 km) per hour. Moving straight east should keep the chasers out of the storm's path—but nothing is certain.

Greg and Bill snap photographs and roll video to use later for scientific study. Soon the wall cloud begins to swirl. Spinning air, also called a **vortex**, is invisible by itself. If it contains cloud droplets or debris, a funnel cloud can be seen. When the funnel cloud comes in contact with the ground, it becomes a tornado.

The chase team cannot see a tornado yet, but that does not mean one is not there. A tornado can be causing damage on the ground even when no funnel cloud is visible. Sometimes a twister is wrapped in rain, making it very hard to spot.

Brown dust and debris are flying up from the ground. The chasers see the tornado! Greg's heart takes an extra beat as he watches the dizzying whirlwind suck up dirt in its path. The dark gray column spins faster, getting tighter and tighter until it looks like a stovepipe. Greg calls in over the ham radio to report the tornado's position to the local weather service office.

The twister grows until it is about 0.25 mile (0.5 km) wide. This is wider than the average tornado, which measures about 50 yards (45 m) across. Amazingly, there is hardly any noise. Because air in motion is silent, a tornado's sound depends on what it hits and what the air is passing through. A twister spiraling across a field sounds like a rushing waterfall, while one

## Shape Shifters

In 1925, the largest single tornado ever to hit the United States cut a 219-mile (352-km) path through Missouri, Illinois, and Indiana. Because the tornado was wrapped in rain, many of the 689 people killed did not see it. They mistook the twister for a harmless rain shower.

*Down the road, the tornado spins at full throttle. This twister has taken on a classic stovepipe shape.*

barreling through metal or wood roars louder than a train engine. Although he has seen more than a hundred tornadoes, Greg never tires of this awesome sight. "It's an adrenaline rush," he says. "Pure wonder, inspiration, and excitement."

As the tornado passes to the west, in front of the Sun, its color changes from dark to light gray. Soon the tornado starts to **rope out**, becoming very skinny before finally disappearing. It is all over. From beginning to end, the tornado lasted 15 minutes, a few minutes longer than most.

For the next several hours, Bill and Greg follow the remaining thunderstorm, taking pictures of the sunset and lightning bolts. By the time they are finished, it is nearly

10:00 P.M. The team has been chasing for 12 hours and is still 3 hours from home base. They are exhausted but thrilled.

Being hit by a tornado is not the main threat storm chasers face. Odds of this happening are low, as experienced chasers know how to keep a safe distance from twisters. Wind, lightning, hail, heavy rain, and **chaser fatigue**—getting very tired—are more dangerous than the twisters themselves. Some chasers have fallen asleep at the wheel after a long day on the road. Bill and Greg play the radio loudly and take turns driving to keep alert.

Today, skill, timing, and patience paid off. Luck was also on their side. As a light rain begins to fall, the chase team turns for home.

*Chasers watch dramatic lightning as they continue to follow the thunderstorm. By now, the tornado has roped out.*

*One of more than sixty violent tornadoes that hit Oklahoma on May 3, 1999*

# Chapter Two

# Outbreak!

Oklahoma City had never been struck by an F-5 tornado, the strongest of all twisters, even though the city lies in the heart of Tornado Alley. Then, on the morning of May 3, 1999, white, puffy cumulonimbus clouds began to bubble in the sky. By late afternoon, strong super-cells were churning out one violent twister after another. From Oklahoma to Kansas, at least one tornado was spiraling along the ground for 6 straight hours.

In all, 78 twisters touched down—65 in Oklahoma alone. The devastation caused $1 billion in damage and killed 48 people. That afternoon, chaser Greg

*Satellite images of the swarm of violent tornadoes. On the left is the actual visible image; on the right is the radar data.*

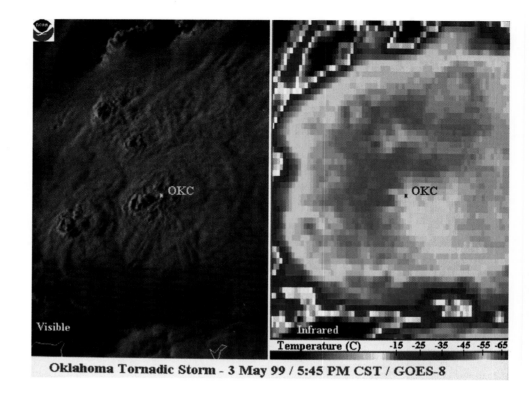

Visible

Infrared

Temperature (C)  -15  -25  -35  -45  -55  -65

**Oklahoma Tornadic Storm - 3 May 99 / 5:45 PM CST / GOES-8**

Stumpf saw 13 tornadoes, including the one that tore through Oklahoma City. This whirlwind packed winds of up to 318 miles (511 km) per hour. More than 3,000 homes and businesses were damaged, and 22 houses were ripped right off their foundations. Forecasters later dubbed the Oklahoma City tornado an F-5, the most powerful on the **Fujita Scale**.

It is difficult to accurately measure the high winds inside a tornado, so scientists rely on the Fujita Scale, or F-scale, for help. Created by Theodore Fujita, the F-scale looks at the damage a tornado causes to figure out its wind speed. Nearly 70 percent of the twisters that hit the United States fall into the F-0 and F-1 categories. These weak tornadoes are typically less than 3 miles (5 km) long and no wider than 50 yards (45 m). They usually do little damage—unless they strike without warning.

About 30 percent of tornadoes are strong tornadoes, rating F-2 or F-3 on the scale. Those reaching F-4 or above are called violent tornadoes. Fewer than one in fifty twisters ever becomes violent, but the most violent tornadoes cause almost two-thirds of tornado-related deaths.

*The F-4 and F-5 tornadoes in Oklahoma caused more than $1 billion in damage and killed 48 people. Only the front door and partial foundation of this house remain standing (at left).*

# Fujita Scale

| Rating | Estimated Wind Speed | Damage |
|---|---|---|
| F-O (weak) | 40–72 mph (64–116 kph) | **Light**: Damage to TV antennae, chimneys, and small trees (about 3 of 10 tornadoes are F-0) |
| F-1 (weak) | 73–112 mph (117–180 kph) | **Moderate**: Broken windows, mobile homes overturned, moving cars pushed off roads (about 4 of 10 tornadoes) |
| F-2 (strong) | 113–157 mph (181–253 kph) | **Considerable**: Roofs torn off, mobile homes and large trees destroyed (about 2 of 10 tornadoes) |
| F-3 (strong) | 158–206 mph (254–331 kph) | **Severe**: Cars lifted off the ground, trains overturned (about 6 of 100 tornadoes) |
| F-4 (violent) | 207–260 mph (332–418 kph) | **Devastating**: Solid walls torn apart, cars tossed, large objects become missiles (about 2 of 100 tornadoes) |
| F-5 (violent) | 261–318 mph (419–511 kph) | **Incredible**: Homes lifted off their foundations and thrown, straw and grass able to pierce tree trunks (fewer than 1 of 100 tornadoes) |
| F-6 to F-12 (violent) | 319–700 mph (512–1,126 kph) or Mach 1, the speed of sound | **Inconceivable**: Though it was once thought tornadoes could reach the speed of sound, scientists now believe F-5 is the top of the scale |

# A Strange Twist

No tornado is quite like another, which is one reason why chasers never seem to lose interest in them. Tornadoes can look like thin needles, thick cylinders, bowls, or no distinct shape at all. A few even have loops in the middle. Some twisters might have more than one vortex circling around a larger main tornado. Tornadoes can even be invisible.

Sometimes a twister takes a straight path; other times it travels in a curved one. Most tornadoes move over land at about 30 miles (50 km) per hour or less, but stronger ones can zip along at twice that speed. A tornado can last for a few seconds or continue for several hours, traveling more than 50 miles (80 km) before it ropes out.

It is a myth that tornadoes cannot cross water or form on it. **Waterspouts** are tornadoes born over water, usually in the warm tropical seas near the equator. Most waterspouts are weak and harmless, but powerful ones can send a column of water 20 feet (6 m) into the air.

*Tornadoes come in many shapes and sizes. Waterspouts, which form over tropical seas, can send columns of water 20 feet (6 m) into the air.*

## Storm Catcher

Photojournalist Warren Faidley captures wild storms on film. He photographs lightning, tornadoes, and hurricanes for books and magazines around the world. His photo *Lightning vs. the Tank Farm* (right) is one of the closest pictures ever taken of a lightning bolt striking something on the ground—Faidley was just 400 feet (120 m) away. Getting good tornado shots is one of Faidley's greatest challenges. Many tornadoes occur at night, so they are impossible to photograph. Some twisters are hidden by rain or dust, and others last only a few minutes. Although he has taken hundreds of storm photos, Faidley is still searching for the ultimate twister.

Tornadoes are sometimes downright weird. In 1877, a twister sucked snakes out of a pond and dropped them on the city of Memphis, Tennessee. Tornadoes with wind speeds above 200 miles (320 km) per hour have been known to pick up cars, cows, and even pianos. In 1990, a monster twister in Illinois lifted a 20-ton truck off the road. In Lubbock, Texas, a tornado once pushed a 45-ton locomotive 150 feet (45 m) along a railroad track. Winds in the most violent of tornadoes can ram blades of grass into wood. A tornado that tore through Saragosa, Texas, in 1987 turned a fork into a torpedo and shot it straight into a tree trunk.

*The powerful winds of a tornado in Saragosa, Texas, drove this fork into a tree.*

Sometimes the objects a tornado sucks up are not damaged at all. The constant airflow inside a vortex allows it to set things down quite gently. People once found a jar of pickles 25 miles (40 km) from where a twister had snatched it, and the glass was not even cracked. Imagine being scooped up by a tornado! That is exactly what happened to seven-month-old Joshua Walls when a late-autumn tornado hit Des Arc, Arkansas, in 1995. It is believed the 190-mph (300-kph) winds, which destroyed his house, carried Joshua the length of almost three football fields. When rescuers finally found the baby in a rice field, he had only minor cuts and bruises.

*A dust devil is a small column of spinning air created when the Sun heats the ground on a hot day. Most dust devils swirl at 25 miles (40 km) per hour or less and usually spin out in a few minutes.*

# Chapter Three

# Into the Twister

Benjamin Franklin might have been the first amateur storm chaser in the United States. It was a hot August day in 1755 when Franklin, riding on horseback through the Maryland countryside, caught sight of a **dust devil** spinning toward him. The thrill of the hunt was too good to pass up. When the 50-foot (15-m) dust devil passed him, Franklin swung his horse around and followed it for nearly a mile. Franklin described his chase as "a real treat."

## Play It Safe

People used to open their windows when they heard a tornado warning because they believed a tornado's low-pressure center would cause their house to explode. Now we know that homes are destroyed by high winds, not low pressure. When a tornado warning is issued, it is best to quickly take shelter in a room with no windows, such as a bathroom or closet, on the first floor of a house or building—and keep all windows closed.

# Taken by Storm

Until 1928, no one had ever survived being hit by a tornado. Scientists could only wonder what went on inside one. They got their answer when Will Keller, a Kansas farmer, found himself smack in the middle of a giant twister.

Keller was taking cover from a storm with his family in their cellar. Just as he was about to shut the overhead door, the tornado passed directly above him. "Everything was as still as death," he later recalled. "There was a strong, gassy odor and it seemed I could not breathe. There was a screaming, hissing sound coming directly from the end of the funnel."

Keller watched as smaller tornadoes formed and broke away from the main tornado. He saw brilliant flashes of lightning zigzagging from one side of the funnel to the other. Keller's glimpse into the center of a twister gave scientists some important clues, but there was still much to learn.

# Chasing Knowledge

In the 1970s, scientists began chasing storms to find out more about how tornadoes work and to learn to predict them. The National Oceanic and Atmospheric Administration (NOAA) formed the National Severe Storms Laboratory to study thunderstorms and tornadoes. In 1981, NSSL researchers built **TOTO (TOtable Tornado Observatory)**, named for Dorothy's dog in *The Wizard of Oz*. TOTO was a 55-gallon (200-liter) drum enclosing about 400 pounds (180 kilograms) of weather equipment. Scientists planned to park TOTO in

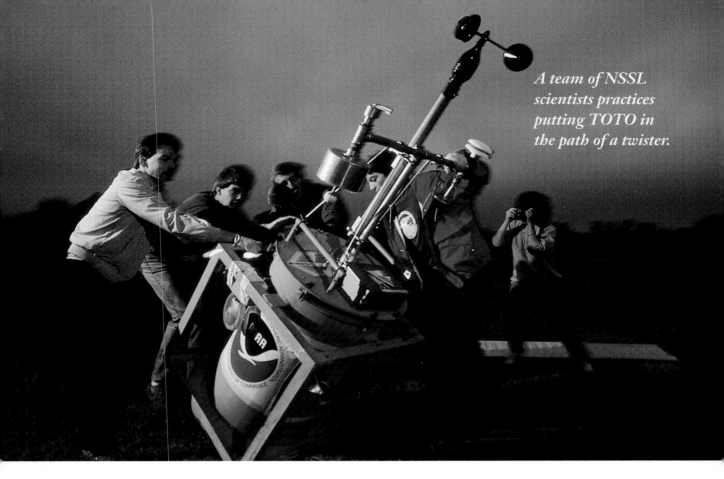

*A team of NSSL scientists practices putting TOTO in the path of a twister.*

front of a twister so that its sensors would pick up weather readings as the whirlwind passed. In the 1980s, TOTO got close to a few tornadoes but never made it into one. Scientists realized it was simply too dangerous to put the drum in the path of a twister, and the project came to an end.

In 1986, meteorologist Fred Brock built a small-scale version of TOTO called the **turtle**. He packed weather sensors into metal casings that looked like turtle shells, then placed them on roads where tornadoes were expected to cross. On May 21, 1991, a tornado came within 1 mile (1.6 km) of four turtles, but no turtle has been inside a twister yet.

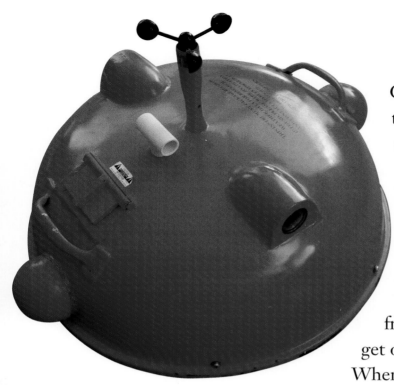

*Dillo-Cam, the first instrument to record the inside of a tornado*

In the early 1980s, physicist Stirling Colgate designed rockets with miniature sensors that could be shot into a tornado. The rockets, which measured air pressure and temperature, had to be blasted from an airplane at the speed of sound to keep from being kicked out of the vortex by high winds. For three years, Colgate tried launching the rockets from his Cessna airplane but failed to get one inside a tornado.

Where other inventions fell a bit short, a video camera finally succeeded. In the mid-1990s, storm-chasing tour guide Charles Edwards built the **Dillo-Cam**. He loaded a video camera inside a 12-by-13-inch (30-by-33-centimeter) fiberglass container and weighed it down with 70 pounds (30 kg) of lead. His goal was to set the camera on a road in front of an oncoming tornado and catch the fury on film.

Edwards's friends thought the new device would never work, but he kept trying. On May 25, 1997, in Perth, Kansas, the Dillo-Cam took a direct hit from a tornado. Mud and debris quickly covered the lens, but the camera kept rolling to record the twister's deafening roar as it passed. Edwards is currently working on his third Dillo-Cam, a smaller, high-tech version of the original.

## Dillo-What?

Less than 6 inches (15 cm) high, the Dillo-Cam was named after an animal that also hangs out near Texas and Oklahoma highways—the armadillo.

# Twister Technology

Today, scientists chase storms in vans packed with the latest in computer technology, cellular phones, weather scanners, satellite dishes, and mobile **Doppler radar**. Doppler radar sends microwave signals into a thunderstorm. The waves bounce off falling rain and hail and send back critical information about a storm's strength and direction.

University of Oklahoma professor Josh Wurman took Doppler one step further by mounting a radar unit on the back of a truck. **Doppler on Wheels (DOW)** lets chasers get within 2 miles (3 km) of a tornado, closer than they have ever been before. In 1997, the addition of a second DOW allowed

*Doppler on Wheels probes a supercell.*

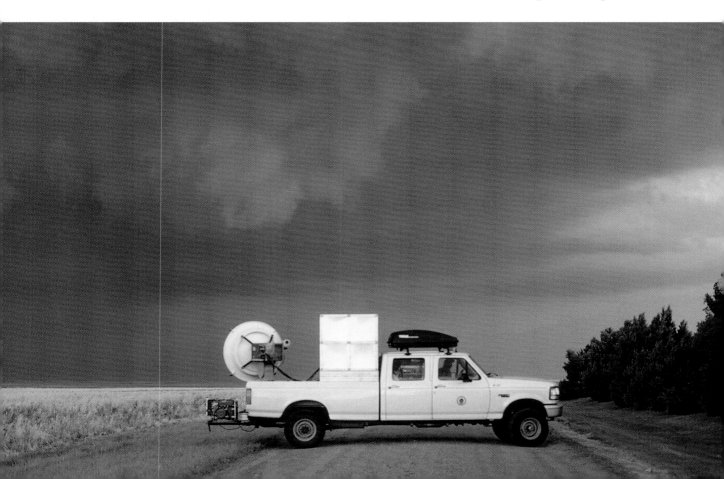

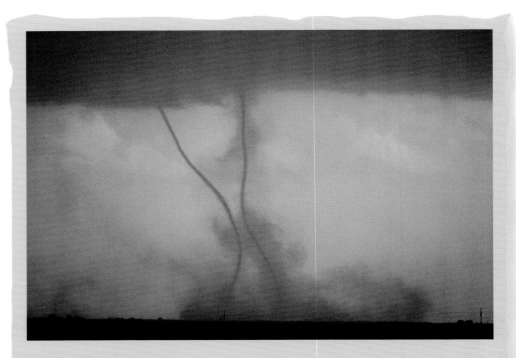

## Without Warning

On May 22, 1987, a multiple-vortex twister touched down in Saragosa, Texas, in the middle of a high-school graduation ceremony. The town, which rarely got major tornadoes, had no Skywarn storm spotters or sirens to alert its citizens to severe weather. In minutes, the F-4 twister destroyed everything in its path. In a population of 183, 121 people were injured, and 30 were killed.

chasers to peer into the same storm from different angles to see it three-dimensionally. During the swarm of tornadoes that hit Oklahoma in 1999, one DOW clocked a wind gust at 318 miles (511 km) per hour, the highest tornadic wind ever recorded.

National Weather Service forecasters rely on weather satellites, radiosondes, and **NEXRAD (NEXt Generation**

**Weather RADar)** to predict and probe twisters. NEXRAD, a network of highly sensitive Doppler radars, tracks large thunderstorms. It can spot a vortex forming and tip off forecasters to a possible tornado.

New research and technology have helped increase tornado warning times from less than 5 minutes 10 years ago to about 12 minutes today. When lives are at stake, every second counts. The average warning time during the May 3, 1999, Oklahoma outbreak was 18 minutes—a major reason, experts believe, why so few lives were lost.

As much as scientists have learned about tornadoes, these violent storms keep far more secrets than they reveal. Although forecasters can predict a severe storm 8 to 12 hours ahead of time, they still cannot tell exactly where or when a tornado will form. They also do not completely understand what triggers an outbreak. Why do some thunderstorms produce tornadoes while others do not? As long as these questions remain, storm chasers will be on the road searching for answers.

*A satellite image of Hurricane Andrew, shown on two consecutive days as it approaches and passes over Florida*

# Chapter Four

# The Hurricane Hunters

Sand castles and red-striped umbrellas dot the sunny beach. A breeze gently ruffles the leaves on the palm trees. It is a perfect summer day on the Florida coast. Hundreds of miles out in the Atlantic Ocean, it is a different story. Warm, moist air is brewing up a thunderstorm. Winds are picking up speed and moving the dark clouds in a counterclockwise motion. A **tropical cyclone** is beginning to form. A tropical cyclone is any rotating storm born over warm ocean waters.

*Hurricane Hunters take measurements aboard their plane.*

There is a very good chance that today's storm will grow into a hurricane.

The Hurricane Hunters are already in action. One of their WC-130 airplanes is heading straight for the storm. The Hurricane Hunters are members of the Air Force Reserve's 53rd Weather Reconnaissance Squadron based at Keesler Air Force Base in Biloxi, Mississippi. Since World War II (1939–45), it has been their mission to fly into tropical cyclones to take weather readings.

On board the plane, computers record wind speeds, temperature, and humidity. A barometer measures **atmospheric pressure**, the weight of air pressing down on Earth. Every 30 seconds, this information is sent to the National Hurricane Center (NHC) in Miami, Florida. Meteorologists there will

use the data to plot the size, strength, and direction of the storm. They issue forecasts and, if necessary, warn the public.

Hurricanes often get their start near the equator, where warm waters and moist air form clouds and thunderstorms. One important ingredient in the recipe for a hurricane is **convergence**, or winds blowing from different directions. The **Coriolis effect**, winds created by Earth's rotation, helps get the storm spinning. Hurricanes can stretch from 200 to 600 miles (320 to 965 km) wide. They sometimes crash onshore, bringing high winds, heavy rains, tornadoes, and a **storm surge**, a rapid rise in ocean waters that can cause serious flooding. Seaside towns need as much warning time as possible to prepare for hurricanes.

*Hurricanes bring high winds, heavy rain, and severe flooding.*

## 'Round the Clock

A typical Hurricane Hunter mission lasts 6 to 11 hours and covers 3,500 miles (5,600 km).

# Flying into the Eye

The WC-130 skims through thin, wispy **cirrus clouds** at the edge of the storm. Soon raindrops begin to pelt the windows, and it gets darker. The plane has reached the **spiral rainbands**, the first layer of the growing hurricane. The ride gets choppy as wind currents increase.

Suddenly the plane jerks, free-falling 1,000 feet (300 m) in near-darkness. The Hurricane Hunters have entered the **eyewall**, the ring of thunderstorms that surrounds the **eye** of the storm. As it draws up warm water to fuel itself, the hurricane becomes a mighty storehouse for energy. The winds in the eyewall, which reach speeds of 50 miles (80 km) per hour, bounce the plane like a yo-yo. A dagger of lightning slices past the wing. The plane is tossed about for several minutes before the wild ride finally ends.

Suddenly, everything is quiet. The winds are still. A ray of sunlight pokes through the clouds. The crew has made it into the eye, the calm center of the storm. The eye consists of air that is slowly sinking, which is why there are no clouds in it (clouds need rising air in order to form). The eye is generally 20 to 40 miles (30 to 65 km) across, but it can measure up to 100 miles (160 km).

Pilots describe being in the eye of a hurricane as similar to standing in the middle of a football stadium. The dark clouds of the eyewall swirl around them like stadium seats. Looking through the hole in the top of the cloud stadium, the pilot sees

**A World of Power**

A large hurricane can release enough energy to supply the electrical needs of the entire world for one year.

clear, blue sky. Down below, raging ocean waves, some as high as 60 feet (20 m), smash into one another.

When the plane reaches the middle of the eye, a crew member releases a **dropwindsonde**, a package of weather instruments. As it parachutes to the sea, this capsule relays temperature, air pressure, wind speed, and other data to the plane. The Hurricane Hunters will fly in and out of the hurricane several times, taking weather readings and launching more dropwindsondes.

*The eye of a hurricane, seen from a Hurricane Hunter airplane*

# Growing Fury

Hurricane Hunters keep careful tabs on winds within the eyewall. Once wind speeds reach 23 miles (37 km) per hour, the tropical cyclone is called a **tropical depression**. If winds reach 39 miles (63 km) per hour, it is upgraded to a **tropical storm**. When winds are clocked at or above 74 miles (119 km) per hour, the storm is officially a hurricane. All hurricanes are rated 1 through 5 on the **Saffir-Simpson Scale**, based on wind speed, storm surge, and pressure. The rating is updated when the storm gets stronger or weaker.

Like tornadoes, hurricanes seem to have a mind of their own. They can change direction quickly or stay in one area for a long time. Perhaps that is why, since 1950, the World Meteorological Organization has been giving them human names. Each year the organization uses a list of names, starting with the letter "A" and continuing through the alphabet. When a storm causes great damage, its name is retired. Camille, the name of the Category 5 hurricane that hit Mississippi in 1969, will never be used again.

In August 1992, Hurricane Andrew carved a path of destruction 1,000 miles (1,600 km) long. The Category 4

Opposite: *Residents of south Florida send a plea for relief after their neighborhood is destroyed by Hurricane Andrew.*

# Saffir-Simpson Scale

| Rating | Wind Speed | Storm Surge | Damage |
|---|---|---|---|
| Category 1 | 74–95 mph (119–153 kph) | 4–5 feet (1.2–1.5 m) | **Minimal:** Some flooding and minor coastal damage |
| Category 2 | 96–110 mph (154–177 kph) | 6–8 feet (1.8–2.4 m) | **Moderate:** Small trees uprooted, mobile homes damaged, flooding in low-lying areas |
| Category 3 | 111–130 mph (178–209 kph) | 9–12 feet (2.7–3.6 m) | **Intense:** Large trees blown down, mobile homes destroyed, some flooding |
| Category 4 | 131–155 mph (210–249 kph) | 13–18 feet (3.9–5.5 m) | **Extreme:** Roofs blown off homes, large buildings damaged, major flooding |
| Category 5 | Above 155 mph (249 kph) | Above 18 feet (5.5 m) | **Catastrophic:** Homes and buildings destroyed, massive flooding |

storm hit the Bahamas and Florida before whirling through the Gulf of Mexico to clobber Louisiana. Andrew's 145-mph (230-kph) winds shredded nearly 80,000 buildings and flipped several F-18 fighter jets at the Homestead Air Force Base in Florida. Hurricane Andrew killed 53 people, left 200,000 homeless, and caused a record $30 billion in damages.

The average hurricane lasts about six days, but some are much longer. Typhoon John, for example, swirled in the Pacific Ocean for a month in 1994. Once a hurricane reaches land or colder waters, it begins to sputter. Without warm tropical waters to feed it, the storm loses its energy source. The eyewall weakens, winds spin down, and the hurricane breaks apart.

## In the Zone

Meteorologists use a variety of tools to forecast hurricanes. Weather satellites measure sea, land, and cloud temperatures and give forecasters information about growing storms. Doppler radar, which picks up the rotation in spiral rainbands, shows when a hurricane might be creating a tornado. NOAA's high-altitude jet, nicknamed Gonzo, flies above hurricanes to map winds and release dropwindsondes. This technology, along with the Hurricane Hunters, has helped improve the accuracy of hurricane forecasting by nearly 30 percent.

Despite improved forecasting, many scientists believe our risk from hurricanes is rising. More people than ever—45 million in the United States alone—live in hurricane zones, and some cities need two days to get residents out of harm's way.

**What's in a Name?**

Storms that are called hurricanes in the Atlantic are known as typhoons in the Pacific, cyclones in the Indian Ocean, and willy-willies near Australia.

In September 1999, emergency crews worked to evacuate three million people before Hurricane Floyd arrived. Florida highways jammed with cars, and traffic was gridlocked for more than 14 hours. Had the storm moved onshore, it probably would have flooded roads and trapped thousands of people.

Fortunately, Floyd just missed Florida's heavily populated coast. North Carolina was not so lucky, however. This Category 2 storm dropped 20 inches (50 cm) of rain on the state, caused massive flooding, and killed 47 people.

*Disaster-relief workers rescue a man from the floods of Hurricane Floyd in Bound Brook, New Jersey.*

Although errors in forecasting have been cut in half in the past several decades, some aspects of hurricanes still baffle scientists. For instance, how does the eye of the storm really work? How exactly do these forces of nature—wind, heat, and water—stir up monster storms? And how does a hurricane choose its path? Unraveling some of these mysteries will allow forecasters to better pinpoint where and when hurricanes make landfall, thereby saving lives. For trained storm chasers such as the Hurricane Hunters, each mission offers a new chance to unlock the secrets hidden deep within the whirlwind.

Staff at the National Severe Storms Laboratory receive a daily weather briefing. You can help meteorologists track storms in your town by becoming a Skywarn storm spotter.

# Chapter Five

# What Can You Do?

Many trained storm chasers say they first became interested in weather at a young age. Perhaps you, too, want to learn more about extreme weather. Your local library and the World Wide Web are good places to search for further information about storm chasers, tornadoes, and hurricanes.

The National Weather Service Web site, *http://www.nws.noaa.gov*, offers links to its forecast offices around the nation. You can also purchase an NOAA weather radio to listen to weather reports in your city. If you live in a tornado zone, you might want to become a Skywarn storm spotter. The National Weather Service can tell you more about the training required.

Everyone who lives in tornado and hurricane zones should have a family emergency plan and a disaster kit. Here are a few items to include in your kit:

- flashlight and batteries
- battery-operated portable radio and batteries
- first-aid kit and family medications
- canned food, water, and manual can opener
- pillows and blankets

For more storm-safety tips, contact your local American Red Cross or the Federal Emergency Management Agency (FEMA).

# Glossary

**anvil clouds**—clouds shaped like a blacksmith's anvil that appear on the upper portion of a thunderstorm

**atmospheric pressure**—the weight of air pressing down on the Earth

**chaser fatigue**—low blood sugar, dehydration, and exhaustion resulting from a long day of storm chasing

**cirrus clouds**—high-level clouds made of ice crystals that appear as thin, wispy, strands

**convergence**—winds blowing from different directions

**Coriolis effect**—winds created by Earth's rotation

**cumulonimbus clouds**—tall, towering clouds that produce thunderstorms and, in some cases, tornadoes; also called thunderheads

**Dillo-Cam**—a video camera housed in a weighted fiberglass case that is placed in the path of a tornado

**Doppler on Wheels (DOW)**—a Doppler radar unit mounted on a truck that allows chasers to closely follow developing storms

**Doppler radar**—a weather instrument that sends out radio waves to bounce off falling rain and hail to determine a storm's direction and strength

**dropwindsonde**—an instrument package attached to a parachute that is dropped into the eye of a hurricane to take weather readings

**dry line**—the boundary between air masses along which thunderstorms and tornadoes are most likely to occur

**dust devil**—a small, usually harmless, whirlwind created by the Sun when it heats the ground

**eye**—the area of low pressure that forms the calm center of a hurricane

**eyewall**—a layer of thunderclouds, heavy rains, and strong winds that rotate around the eye of a hurricane

**Fujita Scale (F-scale)**—a scale that determines the strength of a tornado based on the damage it has caused

**funnel cloud**—a cloud that rotates from the bottom of a storm but is not in contact with the ground (if it touches the ground, it becomes a tornado)

**humidity**—the amount of moisture in the air

**hurricane**—a tropical cyclone with winds at or above 74 miles (119 km) per hour; also called a cyclone or typhoon

**meteorology**—the science of weather

**NEXRAD (NEXt Generation Weather RADar)**—a network of highly sensitive Doppler radars that can peer into thunderstorms and spot the early stages of a tornado

**radiosonde**—an electronic instrument attached to a helium balloon that relays weather data to meteorologists

**rope out**—to take on a ropelike appearance and become thin before disappearing; what a tornado does in the final stage of its life cycle

**Saffir-Simpson Scale**—a rating system that classifies hurricanes based on their wind speed, storm surge, and barometric pressure

**spiral rainbands**—rotating clouds and heavy rains on the edge of a hurricane

**storm chaser**—a person who follows severe storms

**storm surge**—a rapid rise or swell of seawater created by a tropical cyclone's winds

**supercell**—a large, long-lasting thunderstorm that can produce tornadoes

**thunderstorm**—a storm produced by cumulonimbus clouds causing thunder, lightning, gusty winds, rain, hail, and, in severe cases, tornadoes

**tornado**—a violently rotating column of air that extends from the clouds to the ground

**Tornado Alley**—an area of central North America that gets more tornadoes than anywhere else in the world

**TOTO (TOtable Tornado Observatory)**—a barrel filled with weather instruments, designed to be placed in the path of a tornado

**towers**—rapidly growing, cauliflower-shaped cumulonimbus clouds that often bring showers and signal a thunderstorm

**tropical cyclone**—any rotating storm that forms over warm ocean waters, including tropical depressions, tropical storms, and hurricanes

**tropical depression**—a tropical cyclone with maximum winds of 38 miles (61 km) per hour

**tropical storm**—a tropical cyclone with maximum winds of 39 to 73 miles (62 to 118 km) per hour

**turtle**—a package of weather instruments, housed in a small metal shell, that is placed in the path of a tornado to take readings

**vortex**—a spinning column of air in the atmosphere

**wall cloud**—a cloud 1 to 4 miles (2 to 6 km) in width that lowers from the base of a severe thunderstorm, sometimes prior to a funnel cloud or tornado

**waterspout**—a tornado that forms over water

**weather satellite**—a spacecraft that orbits Earth, photographing clouds and taking atmospheric weather readings

**wind shear**—the effect of winds that increase in speed with height, change direction with height, or both

# To Find Out More

## Books

Challoner, Jack. *Hurricanes and Tornadoes*. New York: Dorling Kindersley, 2000.

Galiano, Dean. *Hurricanes*. New York: Rosen Central, 2000.

Kahl, Jonathan D. *Storm Warning: Tornadoes and Hurricanes*. Minneapolis, MN: Lerner, 1993.

Kramer, Stephen. *Eye of the Storm: Chasing Storms with Warren Faidley*. New York: G. P. Putnam's Sons, 1997.

Lauber, Patricia. *Hurricanes: Earth's Mightiest Storms*. New York: Scholastic Press, 1996.

Morgan, Sally. *Weather*. New York: Time Life Books, 1996.

Simon, Seymour. *Tornadoes*. New York: Morrow Junior Books, 1999.

# Videos

*Hurricanes & Tornadoes*, Schlessinger Media, 1998.

*Nature's Fury*, National Geographic Video, 1996.

*Storm of the Century*, TLC Video, Discovery Communications, 1998.

*Tornado Chasers*, TLC Video, Discovery Communications, 1999.

# Organizations and Online Sites

Federal Emergency Management Agency (FEMA)
500 C Street SW
Washington, DC 20472
(202) 646-4600
*http://www.fema.gov/kids*
This government organization offers public assistance for natural disasters. At this Web site, you can track tropical storms, see disaster photos and videos, and learn how to prepare for hurricanes and tornadoes.

Hurricane Hunters
53rd Weather Reconnaissance Squadron
Keesler Air Force Base
Biloxi, MS 39534
*http://www.hurricanehunters.com*
In cooperation with the National Hurricane Center Tropical Prediction Center, the Hurricane Hunters fly into tropical cyclones to study storms. At their Web site, you can find out more about their missions and even take a cyberflight into the eye of a hurricane.

National Hurricane Center (NHC)
11691 SW 17th Street
Miami, FL 33165
(305) 229-4470
*http://www.nhc.noaa.gov*
Based on the campus of Florida International University, this National Weather Service office issues hurricane watches, warnings, and forecasts.

National Severe Storms Laboratory (NSSL)
1313 Halley Circle
Norman, OK 73069
(405) 360-3620
*http://www.nssl.noaa.gov/edu*
This National Weather Service affiliate researches thunderstorms, tornadoes, and other severe weather.

# A Note on Sources

My research into the world of tornadoes and hurricanes led me to scientists at NOAA's National Severe Storms Laboratory and the Storm Prediction Center, both in Norman, Oklahoma, along with the National Hurricane Center in Miami, Florida.

I also read books by noted experts in the field of extreme weather, such as Howard Bluestein's *Tornado Alley: Monster Storms of the Great Plain*; *Eye of the Storm: Inside the World's Deadliest Hurricanes, Tornadoes, and Blizzards*, by Jeffrey Rosenfeld; and *Inside the Hurricane: Face to Face with Nature's Deadliest Storms*, by Peter Davies. Further narrowing my research, I looked to reference material, books written for young readers, video documentaries, and magazine and newspaper sources.

A full exploration of the topic would not have been complete without the firsthand perspective of those who devote their lives to studying severe weather. It was my intent to seek out trained chasers, focusing mainly on those working to advance the cause of science. I am grateful to all the chasers who offered their insights and expertise, especially meteorologist Betsy Abrams of the Weather Channel, Charles Edwards of Cloud 9 Tours, and photojournalist Warren Faidley. Thanks also to Major Michael Odom and the Hurricane Hunters, 53rd Weather Reconnaissance Squadron at Keesler Air Force Base.

Finally, special thanks to meteorologist Greg Stumpf, who so willingly shared his adventures so that we, too, could experience the thrill of the chase!

—*Trudi Strain Trueit*

# Index

Numbers in *italics* indicate illustrations.

# About the Author

As a weather forecaster for KREM (CBS) TV in Spokane, Washington, and KAPP TV (ABC) in Yakima, Trudi Strain Trueit has traveled to schools throughout the Pacific Northwest to share the world of weather with elementary and middle-school students. She is the author of three other Watts Library Earth Science books: *Clouds*, *The Water Cycle*, and *Rain, Hail, and Snow*.

An award-winning television news reporter, Trueit has contributed stories to ABC News, CBS News, CNN, and the Speedvision Channel. Trueit, who has a B.A. in broadcast journalism, is a freelance writer and journalist. She lives in Everett, Washington, with her husband, Bill.

In her career, Trueit has seen a few funnel clouds but only one tornado, which touched down briefly in rural eastern Washington and destroyed a mobile home.